smalllivingspaces

AUTHOR
Arian Mostaedi

PUBLISHERS
Carles Broto & Josep Mª Minguet

GRAPHIC DESIGN & PRODUCTION
Francisco Orduña

TEXT
Jacobo Krauel

PROOFREADING
Monika Camacho

Printed in Spain

smalllivingspaces

Contents

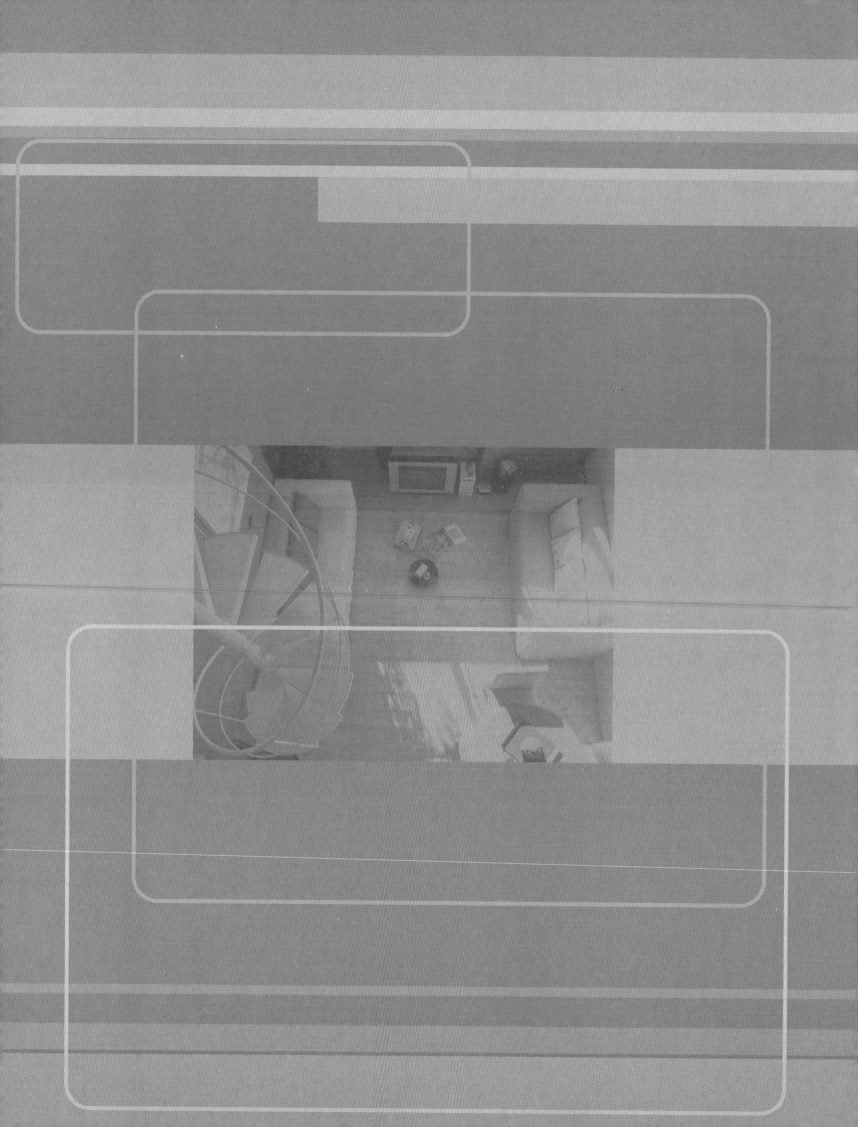

Introduction

Major architectural works are not necessarily those that are measured by the number of square metres. Creation depends on the space and the possibilities that it affords. Therefore, architectural work in small spaces is often a challenge in which one must achieve the seemingly impossible: to turn a small space into a comfortable dwelling in which the lack of living space is not perceived. The aim of this book is to show those works that stand out for their skill in creating stimulating environments in small spaces. This is a complicated task that is not limited to removing partitions, building mezzanines and incorporating specific furniture for the needs of the space. A skilful use of a small space requires far more: one must also think of the requirements and the comfort of the clients, and devise an aesthetic design in which the architecture can adapt to the restrictions of a limited floor area. The designs presented in this book show the solutions and ideas of renowned architects such as the Dutch firm MVRDV, the American Rick Joy, and the Frenchman Jo Crepain, among many others. A total of 32 works show the imaginative force of the designs in which small premises can be transformed into comfortable dwellings, regardless of their original use or location. The designs include apartments created after the division of a large flat, small single-family dwellings in the country, terraced fantasy dwellings and the conversion of an old windmill and a water tower. They are complemented by plans and explanations of the architectural work carried out in each scheme to help the reader understand that creative design does not only depend on the floor area.

Terrelonge
Wedge Profile

Toronto. Canada

The Wedge gallery was a commission which called for two separate but completely complimentary spaces with areas that were partitioned but flowed into one another. The space doubles as an art gallery and a loft. The upper region contains the bedroom, a bathroom which is the private space. The downstairs lower level is a multi-functional public space which houses a spare room, a kitchen, a living room/entertainment area and the Wedge Gallery. The architects decided to play with the space to create tension applying the same techniques as used in graphics. The client's love of music and art is aptly demonstrated in the fixtures, rooms and storage cabinetry that Terrelonge created. To store the

client's over 3,000 CD's the architects created tall 6x3 ft units which would hold music, and an interior "closet" that would house stereo equipment. The fireplace and white wall spaces provide clean surfaces with which enhance the presentation of the art. The materials used to provide textural finishes include sandblasted glass, matte aluminium, brushed stainless steel and poured concrete.

The overall look is comfortable, inviting, complex yet simple. With multi-functionality written all over the space in terms of it being a private space, a public space, a room for entertaining or a room for low key activity.

Photographs: Rico Bella

10

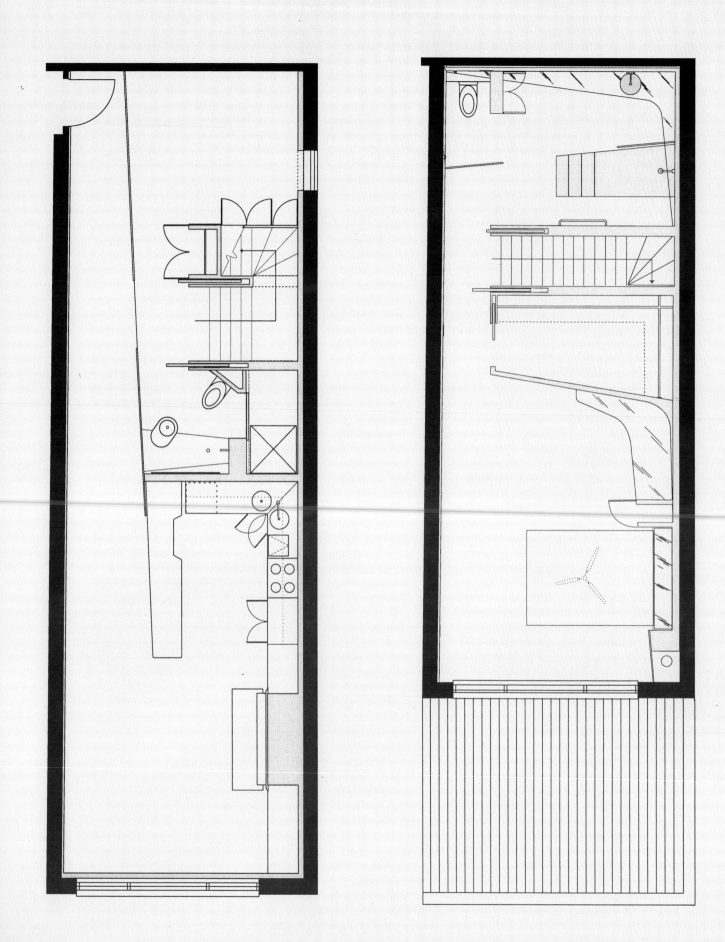

Kar-Hwa Ho
Apartment in New York

New York. USA

The anonymity and light-starved north-facing orientation of one of the many lofts in New York's Chelsea district have been more than remedied in this well considered response to the needs of the client, a bachelor employed in the financial sector. His first requirement —greater unity and definition in the existing layout— is fulfilled by a spatial narrative that creates a marked distinction between the spaces for formal dining and gatherings in the living area, and the tranquillity and quiet of the bedrooms. To accentuate the clean, simple geometry of the space, mouldings, baseboards and trim have been removed and the walls and columns realigned and reproportioned. Removing the suspended ceiling in the living area to expose the continuous structural vaults has added an almost frivolous touch to the design.

The living area is a large single space whose functional divisions are marked by carefully chosen commercial and custom furnishings. The kitchen beyond is custom-designed. The maple credenza with nesting mobile maple units below and frosted glass front and back panels.

The bedroom is dominated by a custom maple platform bed with blanket and pillow storage in its headboard. Two recessed bedside tables with backlit sandblasted glass sides and adjustable glass shelves and reading lamps, all custom designed by the architect. The sunshades accentuate the simplicity of the white geometrical space. The existing oak floor has been stained a darker shade.

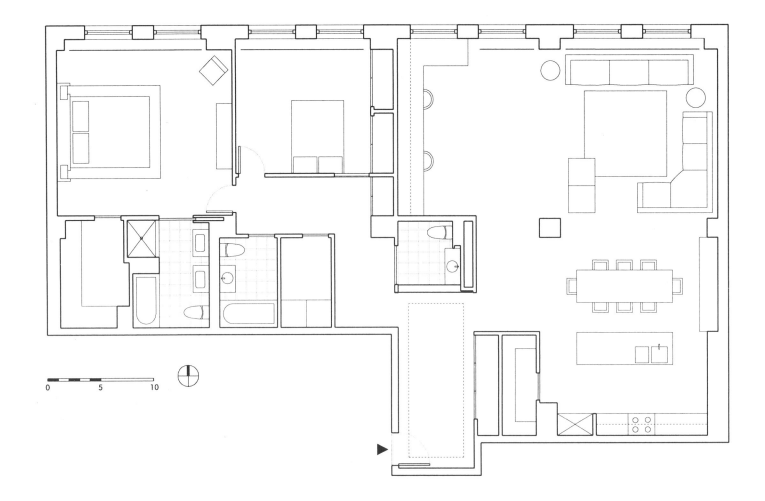

The loft´s atmosphere of calm and repose, enhanced by indirect lighting designed to augment spatial depth, is already evident in the entry foyer.

Sensuous, tactile textures —warm woods, translucent or sandblasted glass, stainless steel— have been used for the furnishings to counterpoint the simplicity of the furniture and spaces.

Eduard Broto
Estudi a l'Eixample

This project by the architect Eduard Broto consisited of rehabilitating an attic located in a Modernista building in the right part of the Barcelona Eixample district. Before the restoration, the attic consisted of a single room used for storage and a large terrace. The scheme made full use of the possibilities of the premises whilst making a minimum number of changes.

The traditional character of the building has been conserved in the transformation of an obsolete space into a modern functional building.

A wooden element similar to a cupboard was created. It separates and organises the different zones into which the dwelling is divided. The generous height of the ceiling made it possible to install a half-floor, thus gaining habitable space.

The living room is situated at the front of the dwelling , and may be fully opened onto the adjoining terrace. The walls and windows of this main room were decorated with the same Modernista floral motif that is found on the stairs of the building. At the rear of the dwelling are the kitchen, bathroom and a small bedroom. All of the rooms are connected to each other, and are separated only by a sliding door system. The bathroom, the most principal zone of the dwelling, was separated from the rest by means of a decorated glazed partition.

Photographs: Eugeni Pons

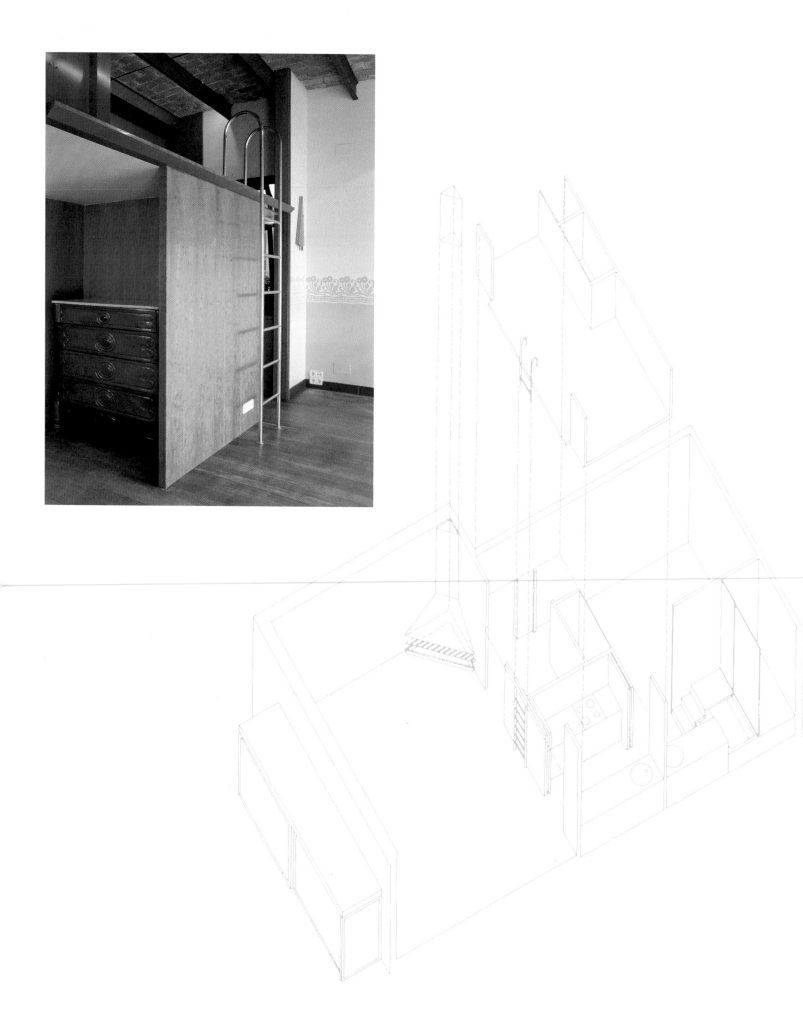

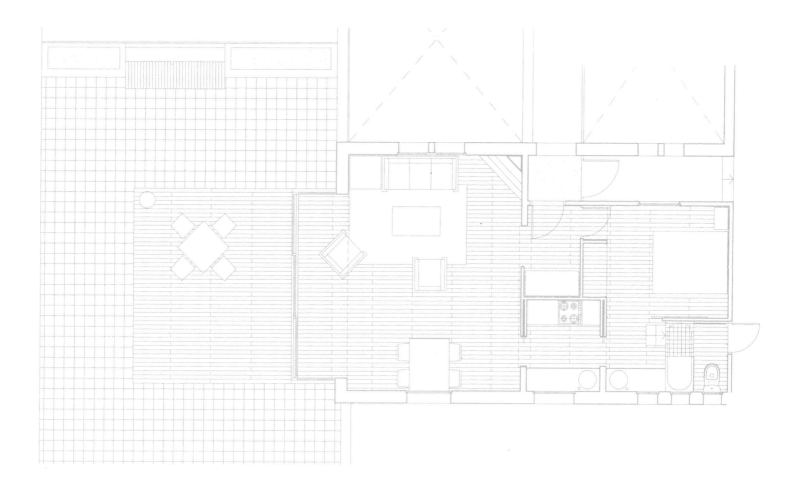

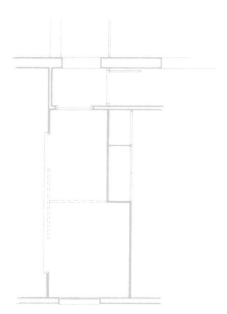

Jo Crepain Architect NV
Water-tower

Brasschaat. Belgium

Until 1937, this water tower with a height of over 23 metres was used to provide water to the castle and other buildings of the county of Brasschat, near the city of Antwerp. After being in disuse for decades due to the construction of four new water tanks and the planning of a modern water supply system, it survived a planned demolition. The conservation of this peculiar cylindrical tower crowned by a large, four-metre-high cistern allowed it to be converted into an unusual single-family dwelling. The architect respected the original industrial typology, leaving the four large pillars that sustain the structure exposed, and also maintained the compositional structure and the essential functionality of the original design. This was achieved by minimising the presence of decorative objects and by limiting the elements and materials to reinforced concrete, structural glass and galvanised metal. Around the original structure, a parallelpiped, double-height volume with a mezzanine surrounds the tower at ground level. This new construction houses the services and a living room that is totally open and transparent to the exterior. This breaks the verticality of the scheme and gains space, and its roof acts as a terrace for the first floor, which houses the main bedroom.

The new tower achieves its maximum expressiveness when it is illuminated at night. The transparency of the glass structure that wraps the building allows the occupants to enjoy the wooded landscape with a small winding creek and reveals the three floors of 4x4 m, each with a small balcony. These floors house, from bottom to top, the study, the guest bedroom and a small winter garden. At the top of the tower the water cistern is conserved, now transformed into a curious space without windows that is intended for private receptions.

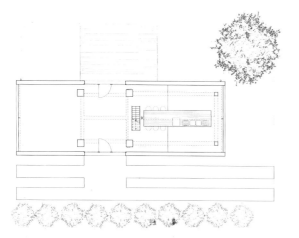
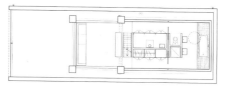
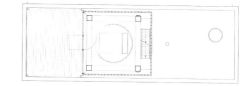

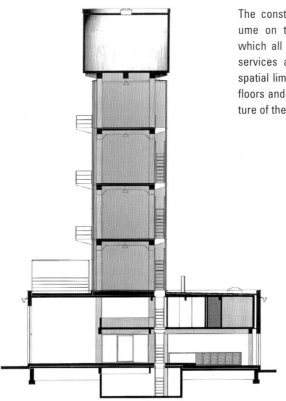

The construction of a larger volume on the first two floors, in which all the common areas and services are housed, breaks the spatial limitation of the rest of the floors and is the most striking feature of the tower.

Luigi Ferrario
Home studio for a graphic designer

Bergamo. Italy

A space with an unusual arrangement, in a traditional ancient Lombard three-storey house, represents the place in which Luigi Ferrario experiments, through a rarefied language, his own vocation for dialogue with old, sedimented forms and materials.

The architectural shell is characterized by a vertical volume of merely seven square meters, used for the bathroom, the staircase, the kitchen below and the sofabed in front of the fireplace, connected above to a work area distributed horizontally with respect to the house.

The domestic space is identified by an entrance at the middle floor, by a covered vaulted staircase connecting a courtyard that does not look onto the studio and to a single living room on the top floor.

The entire design centres on the connection between the entrance and the bathroom, distributed in a single, narrow and vertical environment connected to the attic.

A small opening created when, some time ago, the end of the barrel vault partially covering the original stair collapsed, represents a "natural" cavity of only two square meters providing access to the next floor.

The transformation of the available space has been achieved without disrupting the characteristics of the original structure: the vault, the floor above it in terracotta with inclined steps, the stone masonry.

The introduction of an original structure in iron, glass and wood succeeds in modifying the space and connecting the two floors: through studied additions and minimal subtractions it has been possible to provide for all the functions necessary for domestic life without having to subdivide the available area, so as to obtain space for the indispensable kitchen and bathroom.

Photographs: Alberto Piovano

The bathroom and the small kitchen located on the ground floor are organised to avoid excessive subdivision of the space. As can be seen in this page, the bathroom has a satin-finish sliding glass door.

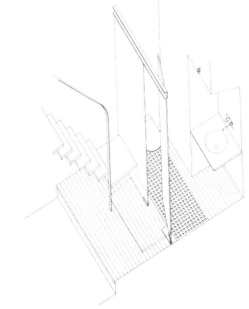

Ian Hay
Hay Apartment

London. UK

Housed in two rooms on the first floor of a modest Georgian terrace off Tottenham Court Road, and occupying only 320 square feet, this apartment was designed around the premise that Hay wanted an spacious house in a very small space. He refused to make the compromises usual in studio-sized flats, such as having a shower instead of a bath, or putting the kitchen in the living room. Instead, he began by calculating the minimum space required to cook, or for a double bed, then looked at ways in which these fnctions could be combined within the limited space. The flat may have everything, but it is not always where you would expect to find it. The bathroom, for instance, is on a plat-

form above the bed, and from the bath, there is a choice of views: you can open up a hatch to watch a small TV beside the bed, or see through the kitchen into the front room. The front room itself doubles as a work pace, with a large table that folds down from the wall so that Hay can run his practice from home. One key to the success of the very tight conversion is the play on transparency. Neither the bathroom nor the kitchen are treated as enclosed rooms, and surprising sightlines run through the flat, so that the claustrophobic feeling associated with tight, boxed-in spaces is avoided.

Photographs: Richard Glover

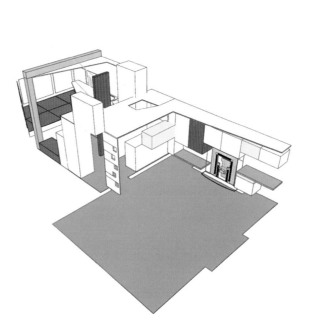

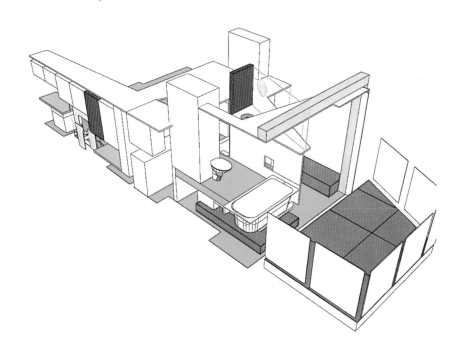

From the bathroom there is a full view of the bedroom and, through the kitchen, of the main bedroom located at the end.

Torsten Neeland
House of Dr. Shank

Hamburg. Germany

The building, which dates from the beginning of the century, contains an apartment and a doctor's clinic in the centre of Hamburg.

The interior, where both areas are connected, was fully redesigned to optimize the spacial limitations.

An important aim was to keep the furnishing at the lowest possible limit in order to allow the space to display its entire beauty. Further open space was created by tearing down a separation-wall between the library and living-room. In this way the architect wished to create a calm environment in which it is easy to concentrate on work and to enjoy the space. Special attention was paid to the lighting of the apartment, wich is of great importance to Neeland and is used as as integral part of the architecture. He belives that it has a magical quality, that it can be used to totally change the atmosphere, and that without light architecture is nothing. The rooms are mostly illuminated indirectly, for example from behind sliding window shades. The flexibility of the shades provides different dimensions of brightness, increasing the perception of space in a limited area.

The light penetrates the rooms indirectly thanks to mobile panels that filter it and bathe the rooms in a very intimate atmosphere.

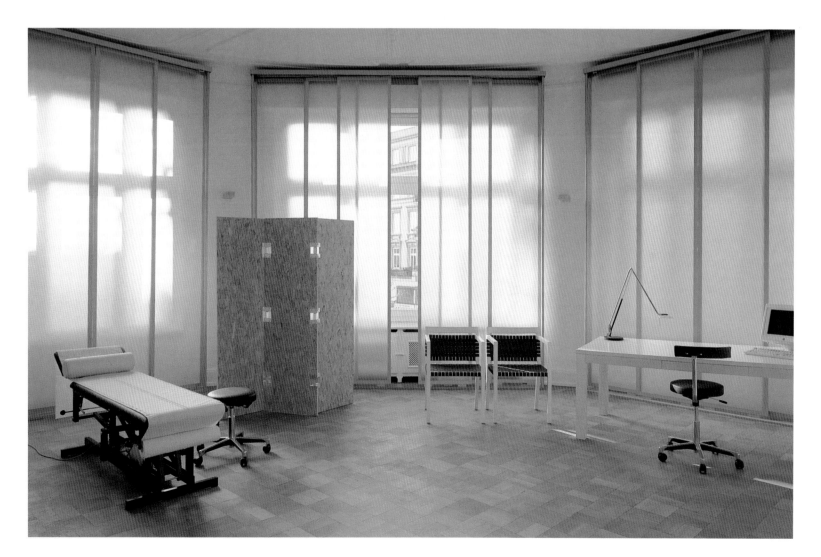

Simon Conder & Associates
Flat conversion in Primrose Hill

London. UK

The client, a barrister with her family, wanted to renovate and enlarge her late 19th century house and patio located in north London. The conversion work was to be undertaken in stages as the resources allowed.

The first stage of the project involved the creation of a private space for the client at the top of house, which would exploit both the unused roof space and the fine views to the rear.

This initial objective was achieved by replacing the original roof with a new steel-framed structure, which incorporated a full width rooflight at the rear. Below this new roof a steel framed sleeping gallery was inserted with toughened glass ballustrad-

ing and a simple staircase in stainless steel and oak.

Bellow the gallery there is a freestanding translucent oval, containing the bathrooms central location provides a degree of separation between the study area at the rear and the living space at the front of the plan. At night the internally lit glass oval provides the primary light source for the space as a whole.

Materials include painted plaster walls and ceilings, oiled oak floors, sandblasted toughened glass for the walls of the bathroom, teak duck-boarding over an oval fibreglass shower tray for the bathroom floor, and stainless steel for the ironmongery, the support structures in the bathroom and the sanitary fittings.

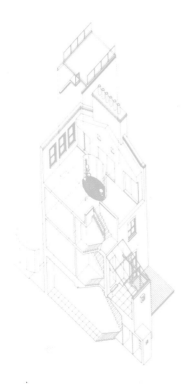

Oswald Mathias Ungers
Wasserturm

The original tower dating from 1957 had only the two upper floors, housing the water tank and machinery, and a high entrance hall. The kitchen floor is a new addition, and is overlooked by a gallery running parallel to the stairs. On the first level it is a newly constructed element containing the bedroom with shower, bath and fitted cupboards. The top floor is a tall space with four windows: sparsely furnished, it is a meditation area with breathtaking views over the Eifel Mountains.

As one enters to the tower one is struck by the succession of spaces that have been created: the alternation of wide-narrow and high-low. Emerging from the low, narrow stairwell there is always a high, wide space with a view of the landscape. The spaces in the water tower are simple elements stacked one on top of the other, but the art of the design lay in the adapting and refining the existent aesthetics to the new use. The spaces and materials are thus left in their purest form: sandstone, the circular form of the steps, the verticality of the layout, the new additions -all is pure, unobtrusive, natural.

An example of this is that the windows largely follow the original design, serving less an idea of living space and views, and more the original purpose of illumination: one window on the stairwell, one in the kitchen and one in the bathroom. However, on the second floor the situation is different. Four windows point in the four directions, thus adding a new dimension to the circular plan thanks to the conceptual rigour of the architect, who pursued the maxim "less is more" with laudable sensitivity.

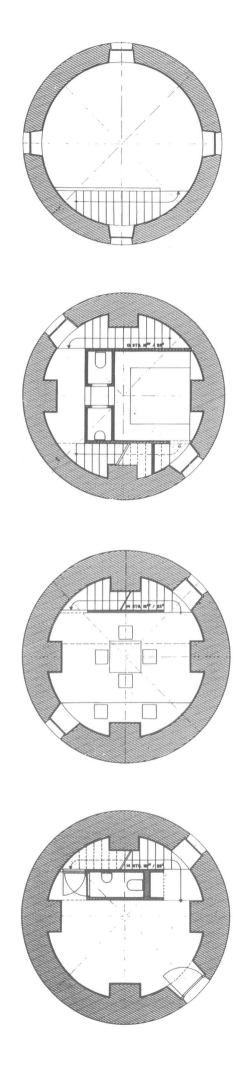

Martin Wagner
Apartment Casa Sorée

Carona. Switzerland

In the renovation of Casa Soree, each of the three apartments occupies a single floor, and the house's three ground-level cellars from a single apartment.

Carona's covered streets and porticoes have been restated in an interior street which connects the three existing storage cells.

This street extends directly from the ground-floor apartment's main entrance, making the apartment's organisation immediately apparent upon entry and and allowing and extended view through the space.

Folowing Ticino tradition, the entry door opens into the kitchen. A new opoening joins the kitchen to the existing covered porti-

co for outdoor dining. The second of the apartment's three rooms, used for living, opens to the pre-existing axis, which runs from the fireplace in the back wall outside.

The third room, for sleeping, includes a bathroom enclosed by a high, free-standing concrete wall which provides privacy and houses the necessary plumbing.

The design draws upon Carona's history and built form and takes advantage of opportunities inherent within the existing structure to develop a unique architectural situation for dwelling.

Photographs: Reiner Blunck

The night area has its own entrance from the garden and includes a bedroom and a bath. The bathroom is enclosed within a bare concrete load-bearing wall which closes on itself and is separated from the roof by an almost imperceptible glass strip.

Joan Bach
Loft Gràcia-2

Barcelona. Spain

This maisonette, remodelled by the architect Joan Bach, is located in a building in the Gracia district of Barcelona.

The scheme is composed of a large, double height living room, an open kitchen and a side area that is developed on three levels. The lower level houses the dining room, the staircases and a bathroom. The middle level houses two auxiliary rooms —a dressing room and a toilet— and the main bedroom, which is visually connected to the living room and accessed through the bathroom. The upper level is independent and houses the two children's bedrooms, a bathroom and a studio/playroom.

It was decided to paint all the walls in a yellow tone that made the space brighter and helped to create a warm atmosphere. With this treatment an interesting chromatic contrast was achieved between the yellow painted surfaces and the flooring, the beams, the staircases, the air conduits, the kitchen and even the picture frames, finished in dark brown tones.

The materials, the finishes and the furniture form a very welcoming space. The lighting is artificial and was designed to create an atmosphere of tranquillity that helps to transmit the sensation of warmth desired by its inhabitants. The floor is made of wood, and the furniture is contemporary and functional.

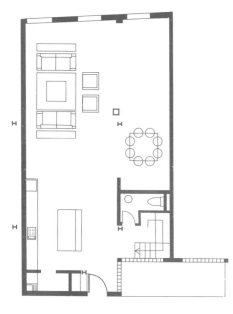
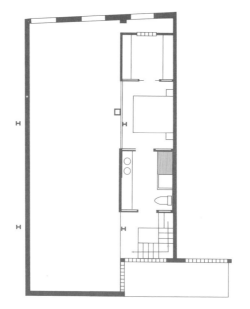
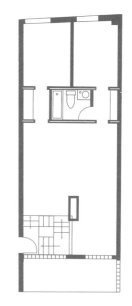

Although they are on different levels, the main bedroom and the living room maintain a visual communication. The peculiarity of this bedroom is accentuated by the fact that it is accessed through the bathroom.

A chromatic relationship has been established between the yellow painted walls and the elements that are set in the space, which are dark brown.

Francesco Venezia
House in Posillipo

Napoli. Italy

The Neapolitan architect´s subtle approach, based entirely on the topographical and cultural interpretation of the site, is expressed in this small but very detailed project. A cautious but decisive touch lends impact to a domestic interior where functions are concealed behind forms.

The house stands on a white cliff in Posillipo, occupying a level terrace along a stairway linked to a seaside roadway half way up the coast.

The house existed already and only interior alterations were made. A wooden shell shapes the cavity forming the entrance area-living room space, onto which the minute entrance opens together with the kitchen and bedroom.

The wooden walls of the ground floor accommodates a wardrobe and cupboards.

The windows as well as the door onto the small balcony on the size facing the sea have deep jambs. The bathroom is at the opposite side of the entrance, excavated in tufa stone. Set in relief within the wall abutting the rock is a recessed fossil of a palm tree.

Photographs: Mimmo Jodice

The photographs on this double page show the small entrance hall seen from the zone housing the living area, the main room of the living.

Gray Organschi
Tennis House

Tennis House forms part of a large forest area in the north-west of the state of Connecticut. The building is located at the end of a small valley, on a site that was formerly a gravel pit but now, after the discovery of an underground spring, is occupied by a pond surrounded by wild grasslands.

In the design of this property the architects aimed to negotiate the relationship between the qualities of the site and the creation of a garden, in which a tennis court is the main feature.

Because the lands at the end of the valley were protected by recent environmental regulations, the habitable spaces of the building had to comply with the legal limits. However, the clients presented an ambitious scheme that included two dressing rooms, a bathroom, service rooms, a kitchen with utility room, a pantry, a bedroom with bunks and a living room at the level of the tennis court. The court has retaining walls made of concrete blocks on three of its sides, leaving open the side furthest from the dwelling with views of the pond. Clover and vetch were planted up to the edges of these walls, giving lightness to ele-ments that tend to offer a very solid appearance. The tennis court looks as if it had been cut cleanly out of the land, and is aligned at the same level as the surface of the pond. Overlooking the court at its south end, the dwelling is embedded into the hillside. The concrete retaining wall that forms the building's back elevation transforms along its lenght to create an exterior shower, a sink counter for the bathroom, a storage wallcontaining the kitchenette and laundry, a rear staircase, an interior fireplace and exterior grill, and ultimately a catch basin fot the roof's rainwater runoff.

Along the facade facing the tennis court, ten columns and a "box" of cypress wood that contains the dressing rooms and the indoor shower support the roof, which is trapezoidal and has a low corner from which the rainwater can drain off. This roof was covered with vegetation, forming a pure plane of grass that is only interrupted by the chimney and a skylight that illuminates the dressing rooms.

The dwelling is articulated around the tennis court and the pond, so from the main living areas, such as the living room and the terrace on the upper floor, one can enjoy the views or watch a tennis match.

George Ranalli
K-loft

New York City. USA

This project is for the renovation of a loft in New York City for two artist and their son.

The existing space was a room with exposed brick bearing walls running the lenght of the space and a brick ceiling with a series of vaults spanning steel sections from the front to the back of the loft. The plan called for two new bedrooms, a new master bathroom, a new kitchen, and a second bathroom. It was also the owner´s intention that the feeling and quality of the original loft be maintained.

The solution as built features a series of volumes sitting in the loft which allow the space of the room to be continuous. Each of the volumes takes a key position so that it contains space as well as producing space between the forms. The elements are made in plaster which then have some fixed translucent glass inserted in the blocks. These glass openings are meant to allow the passage of light and space from one room to another. The corners are protected with large panels of of birch plywood cut in irregular profiles that gives an expressive value to these volumes. These panels are fixed to the plaster walls with a pattern of screw fasteners. All doors, lamps, cabinets, and other decorative objects are custom-designed as part of the project.

The project was designed and built in materials of a high finish to accentuate and contrast the rough container of the existing brick room. The main structure and surface of the new elements is frame and skimcoat gypsum board that gives a smooth, durable finish to the new shapes.

Photographs: Paul Warchol

To maintain the impression of a single open space, the architect has implanted a series of isolated volumes in which the most private rooms are located. Thus, thanks to the constant presence of magnificent vaulted ceramic ceilings and red brick walls, the sensation of continuity is constant.

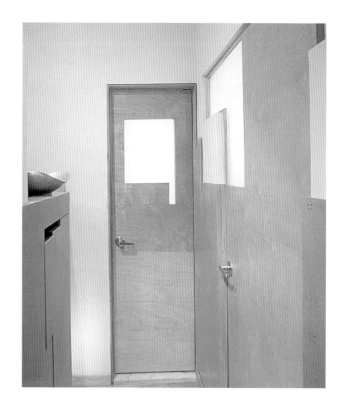

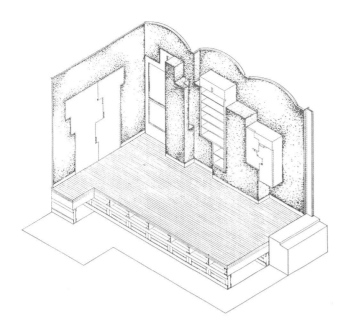

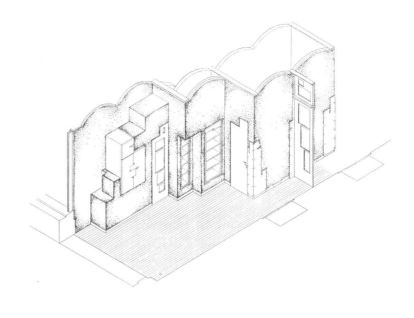

Claesson, Koivisto & Rune
Apartment in Stockholm

Stockholm. Sweden

The task of confronting this team of three architects was how to create a comfortable, uncluttered living space in a very small area.

The apartment, located in the centre of Stockholm, has a total floorspace of just 33,5 square metres containing basically one open-plan room, with adjoining concrete-tiled terrace and blue mosaic-tiled bathroom, connected to the main room by a small opening with a sliding acid-etched window.

In spite of its size, the apartment has all the necessary conveniences. Non-living space storage, dishwasher, refrigerator, freezer, microwave and so on is either built-in or concealed behind doors, resulting in a serene and minimalist aesthetic in which to carry on domestic life. Although the work of several designers has been used in the finished project, all the built-in furnishings were designed by the architects themselves.

The terrace furniture can easily be lifted inside for occasions demanding more seating space, and the futon bed doubles up as a sofa. All the lighting and two motorized Venetian blinds are controlled from one centrally placed panel. The Venetian blinds, when shut, hide both the windows and the work desk.

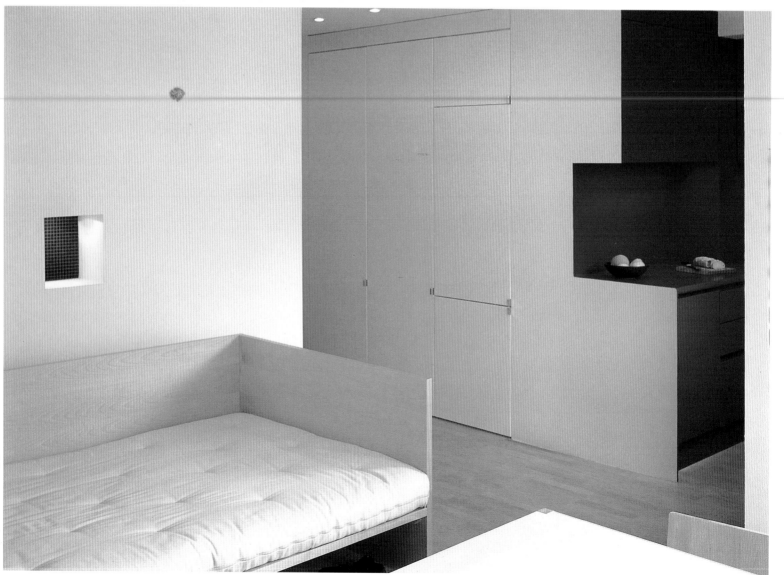

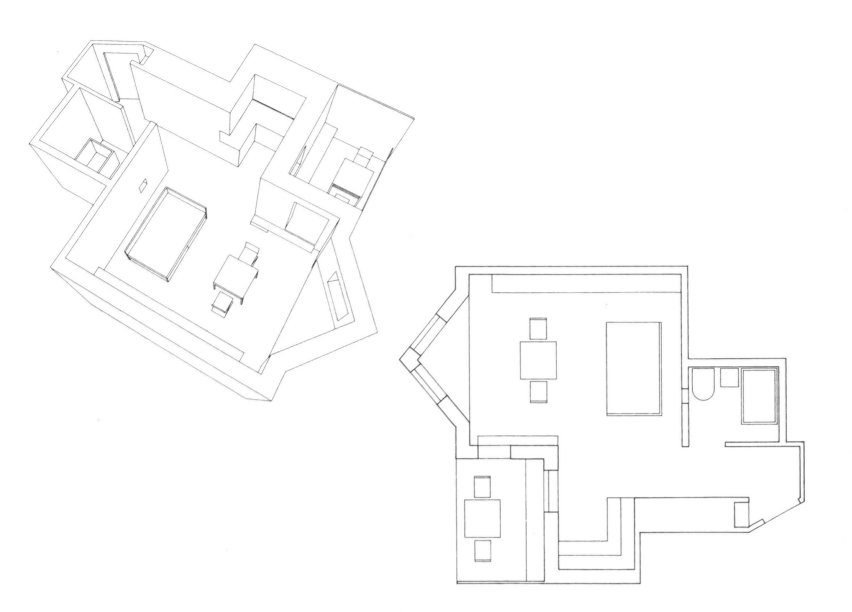

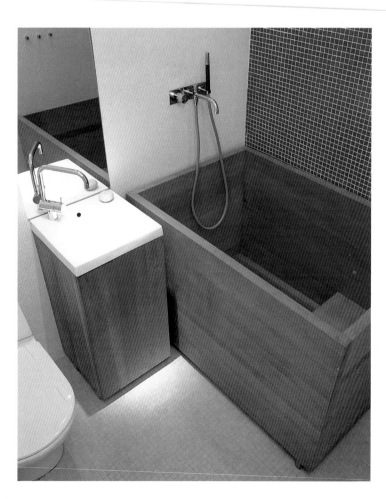

The dwelling is ordered around a small single room, but the architects have managed to give the apartment full visual and spatial opening.

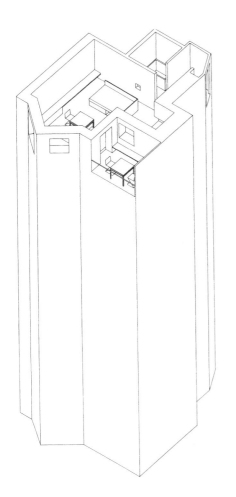

Marco Savorelli
Nicola´s Home

Milan. Italy

A bet was made between the client and designers: to start from zero, working in abstract on "home system" functions and utilities, beginning from recuperation of an unitarian, primary, elementary space, translating old function into new, mitigated and simplified forms.

Discrete presence, operative spaces like bathroom, kitchen and wardrobe translate themselves into monolithic volumes that, reduced into simple forms, gain plastically authority creating new ways, background, bonds and articulations of the perceptive space system.

This is a project where the historical memory of the site meets rigorous formal research, resulting in a well balanced experimentation with new spaces preserving the existing quality of light. The result is a playful alternation of volumes and moods, a fluid exchange between the existing and the designed space. These are characteristics of a project which evolved from the intense dialogue between the architect and the client, aiming to achieve a minimalist aesthetic and at the same time volumetric and functional complexity. This is not a mere operation of interior decoration but the creation of volumes to be lived in and to "live with" in a completely modern and innovative way. The space acquires both a jocose and a reflexive quality.

When entering this apartment the visual impact is instantaneous —a nearly flash-like perception of the space— which reveals the equilibrium between matter and light. The natural daylight traces delicate designs on the neat surfaces, shadows in perpetual movement creating a simple and primordial game of light and darkness.

Photographs: Matteo Piazza

Light was treated as an element of the construction whose function lies not only in lighting the dwelling but also in defining spaces inside it. In this sense, the strategic arrangement of top lighting gives the environment a very distinctive vertical dimension.

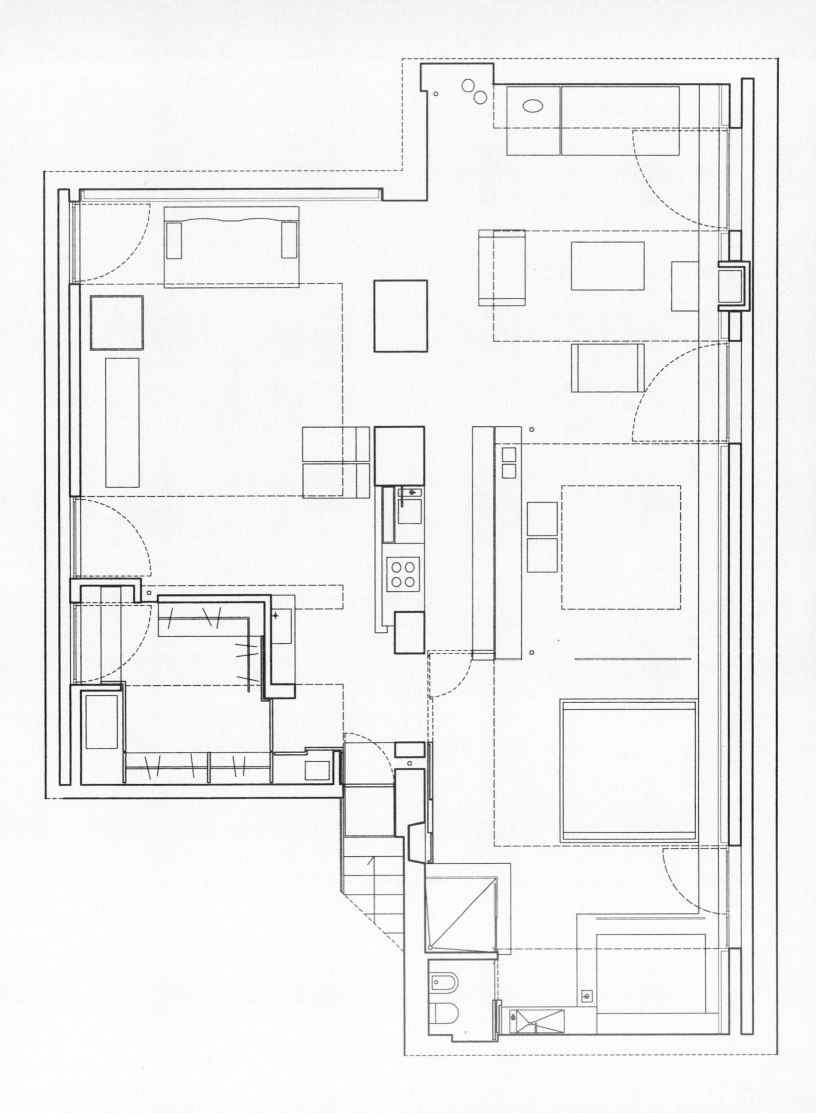

The distribution of spaces follows an open plan, with minimum partitions and a constant search for fluency and dialogue between the different environments. The use of a limited range of materials contributes to this objective.

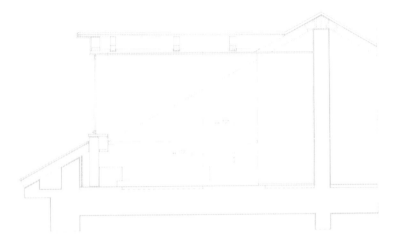

Calvi Merlini Moya
Apartment in Milan

Milan. Italy

Every aspect of architecture questioned afresh, pros and cons of construction newly weighed in the balance, each proposed gesture and feature examined in depth, interior design reformulated as equipping a home so that interior design means "how to make architecture", not "how to furnish spaces". To achieve these aims, Luisa Calvi, Mauro Merlini and Carlos Moya literally started with a *tabula rasa*. The original layout of the late 1950s apartment has been totally remodelled: the structure has been freed up, the traditional corridor has been eliminated, rooms have been redesigned. And the circulation —the heart of the newly extended, efficiently syntaxed, rhythmically disjoined home— has been reinvented as a continuos sequence of visual surprises, a syntax conveying a mood of instability, a calculated uncertainty, a sense of impermanence. In short, the heal-ing virus of doubt has been injected into the concept of living. Horizontality of space, channelled and emphasised by numerous outward-leading sight-lines, is highlighted by materials like ribbed wood fitted with its grain lying horizontal. Reduced portions of colour frame or serve as backdrops to precise architectural features. The spectrum of greys in the central masonry nucleus —lighter in the circulation routes, darker in the partitions and structural spines— contrasts with the white of the external box. Materials are chosen and worked to convey emotions as well as perform satisfactorily. The brushed finish of the Douglas pine and larch doors is hard to describe: you have to touch, open, rotate and slide the various (unconventional) doors that design the space.

Photographs: Andrea Zani

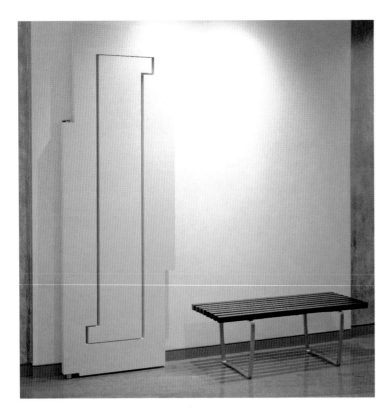

View from the entrance of the dining area enclosed within an ovall
formed by two "comma-shaped"
bleached maple screens.

99

All the perimeter walls are finished with white marmorino, those of the central core in various shades of grey. Lighting with sunken spots, and flooring with American cherry-wood floorboards.

MVRDV
Borneo House

Amsterdam. The Netherlands

In Borneo (Sporenburg) one dwelling stands out for its masterful resolution of the problems of limited space.

Located on plot 18, this apartment is 4.2 metres wide and 16 metres high and has a terrace of double height in the facade giving onto the canal. Initially the regulations only allowed the construction of three floors, a high floor at street level and two more above it. Despite this, the architects were able to build four floors by building in blocks and setting one of the four levels at the rear. A long traverse section was also designed with two "closed" elements: a space with direct access to the street that serves as a garage, and another block suspended over the

terrace and the water on the second level that stands out from the rest of the building and houses the bedroom and a bathroom. The remaining irregular spaces of the house —the kitchen-dining room, the living room and the study— are communicated so as to provide a fluid and simple transition from one room to the next. The rooms were designed with different heights and degrees of privacy. Each one is directly connected to the exterior through an exclusive access, with a double height terrace, an overhanging window and a roof garden aligned with the rear facade.

Photographs: Nicholas Kane

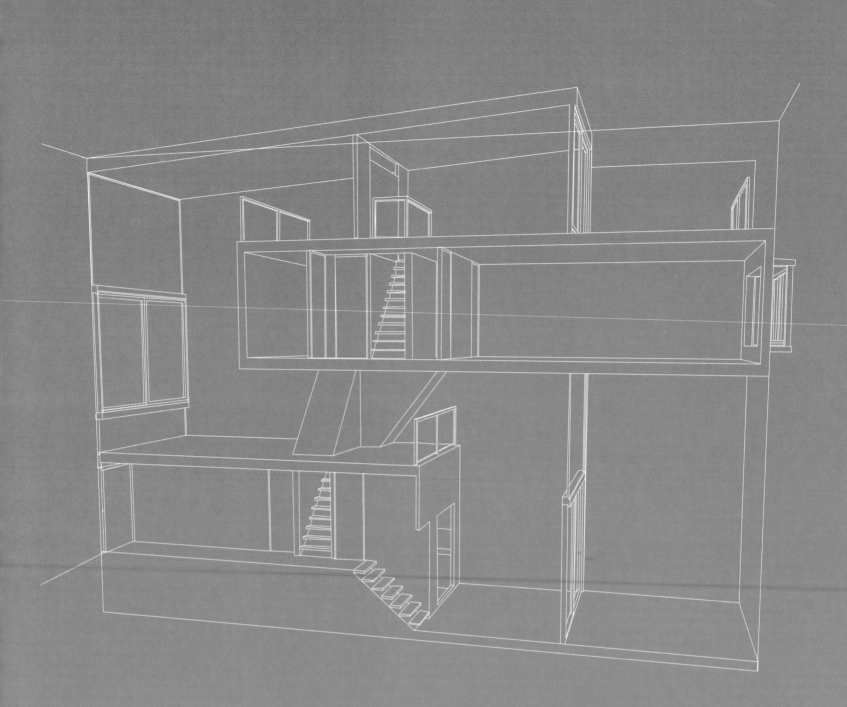

The use of displaced volumes gives this dwelling a large, double-height space, half of which is a covered terrace looking onto the canal.

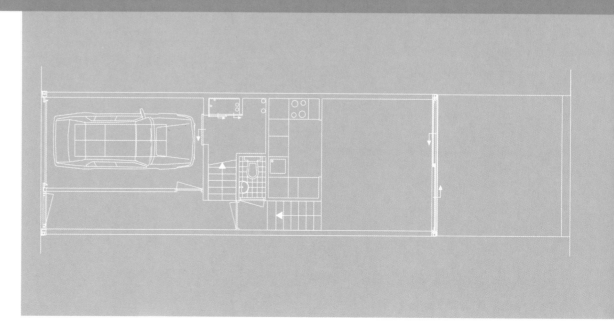

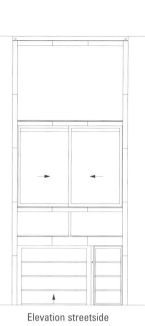

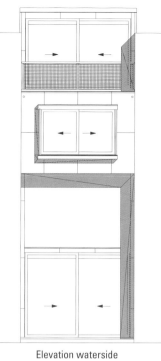

Elevation streetside

Elevation waterside

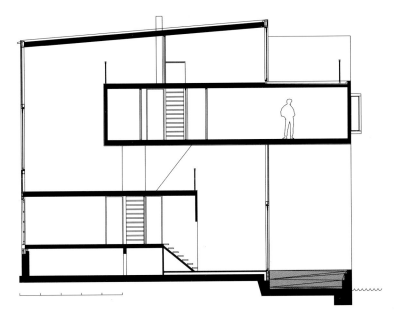

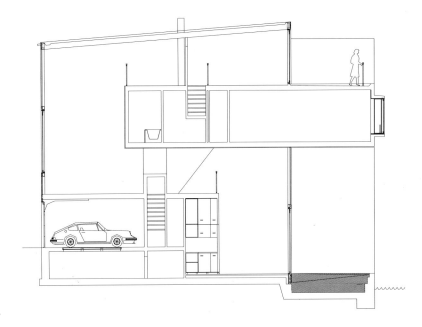

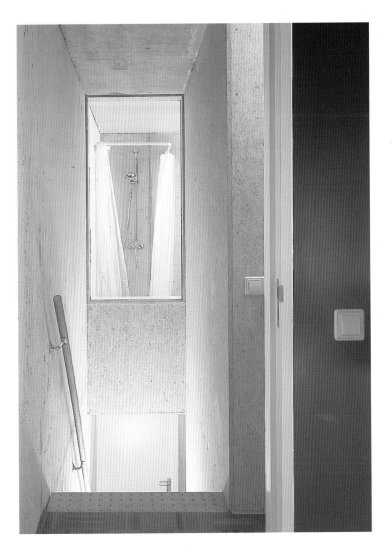

Simon Conder & Associates
Residential conversion of a fire station

London. UK

The clients had bought the top two floors of the redundant Holland Park Fire Station.

Although the building was in a quiet tree lined street; the actual accommodation consisted of a number of small, badly lit rooms with those at the back overshadowed by a mews property only 3.5 metres away from the rear wall.

The depth of the plan combined with the relatively small windows meant that the centre of the plan was particularly dark. The clients' main objective was to find an imaginative way of transforming this rather depressing environment into a light and exciting new home, which would have a generosity of scale and spirit. At more detailed level they wanted a solution that would incorporate an open plan living area, the heart of which was to be the

kitchen, a large main bedroom with an en-suite bathroom, two smaller bedrooms (one of which was to double as a study), an additional bathroom, and a large amount of built-in storage for clothes and their collection of records and compact discs.

At the level of the roof there were dramatic views out over West London and it was clear that the building could be transformed in this rooftop potential could be exploited to create an additional living space and let natural light down into the centre of the deep spaces below.

The final solution was based on three key elements: a roof top conservatory, a flight of stone steps and a three-storey storage wall.

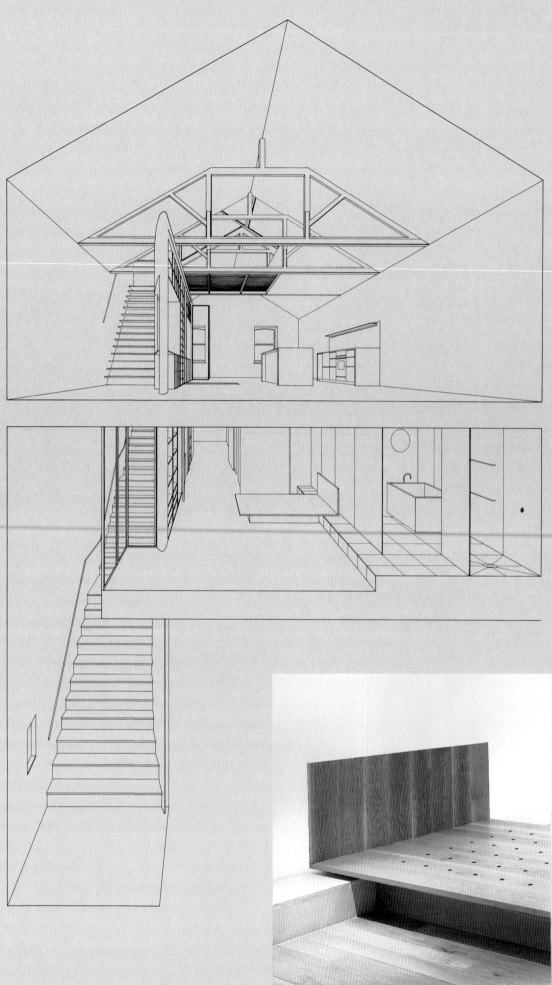

Marc Guard
Apartment in Bankside Lofts

London. UK

This apartment presented several problems. The client's requirement for two bedrooms, as well as the desire to maximize the living area, was complicated by the relatively low ceiling heights. The only means of providing a satisfactory double-height space was by combining the sleeping platforms with another function.

The master bedroom therefore sits above the dressing area, accessed through a large pivoting door. The guest bedroom, adjacent the main entrance, is atop the guest bathroom. The circular stainless steel shower extends into the main living area and provides a sculptural counterpart to the more geometric forms of the master bedroom, with its Z–shaped bed head. A stone clad staircase provides the route up to the guest sleeping platform, optimizing the floor space in the main living area.

The split-level stone bathroom is positioned halfway between the dressing room and the master bedroom above. To allow light from the window in the bathroom to serve both the bedroom and the bathroom; the latter is open plan. However, as the bathroom is on a lower level, it is not visible from the bedroom, and so the perception of space in the bedroom is uncreased.

A large sliding canvas screen can be drawn across the main space, effectively sealing the master bed area off from the living space. The apartment was designed to adapt easily to forthcoming developments in entertainment technology. A compartment has been let into the suspended ceiling in order to take a television projection unit, which will project onto a large 5x3 m sliding screen. In the master bed area, a space has been designated for a flat screen television, enabling new technology to be seamlessly integrated into the apartment with minimum disruption.

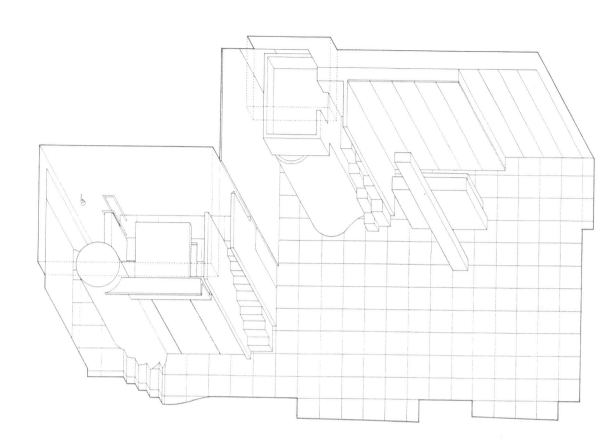

A cicular stainless steel washbasin is attached to th wall of the raised bedroom. The mirror above the washbasin can be adjusted to a number of positions, and conceals a small bathroom cabinet.

Rick Joy
Convent avenue studios

Tucson. USA

The architect Rick Joy designed two modern apartments whilst respecting the historic setting of a desert climate and simple building materials. Thus, two new dwelling spaces were designed as a simple structure evoking the rustic nature of adobe with a traditional construction system.

Starting with simple shed forms that could fit like jigsaw pieces on a small parcel of land, Joy developed a wedge-shaped plan for the houses. The wedge also opened up outdoor spaces between units that could be used as private courtyards that helps to maximize the reduced zones of the apartments.

Although building codes allowed the architect to place the houses along one property line, Joy set them back to allow north- and south-facing windows and to create the courtyards. Inside the houses, the thick walls are the dominant feature, complemented by rough-sawn Douglas-fir roof beams, concrete floors, fir ceilings and windows.

Sunlight is treated as a precious commodity, almost totally blocked on the east and west, and brought in through a narrow skylight above the bedroom and through windows that frame tight views of courtyard.

The organisation and layout of the different zones of these dwellings was designed simply, taking into account the limited space. A fluid communication was chosen between the kitchen and the living room, which are separated only by a counter with the hob that is also used as a table. A mezzanine, which is accessed by a staircase set against the wall, provides an additional environment which is semi-concealed behind bookshelves.

Fotografías: Rick Joy

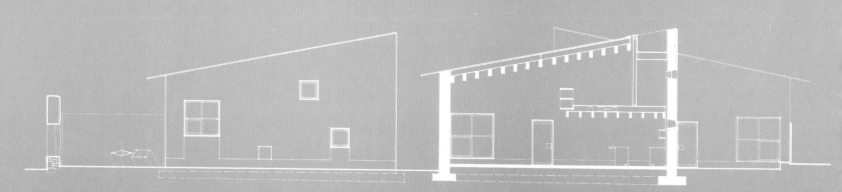

The interior of the dwelling was organized so as to leave a double height and well-lit space for the study area.

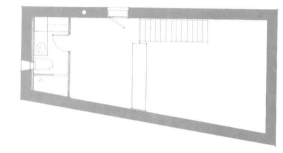

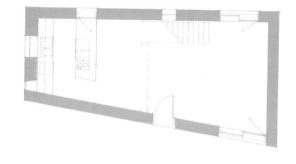

Arnaud Goujon Architecte DPLG
Transformed penthouse

Paris. France

In the heart of Paris, the architect Arnaud Goujon transformed an old greenhouse located at the top of a block of flats into a small and comfortable refuge with a terrace and unique views. Conceived as an extension of the loft apartment, this volume would soon become the favourite room of this home. It is a scheme in which the initial volumetrics was respected and a new wooden frame was superimposed on the steel structure. On the exterior, the shingle boards are made of red Canadian cedar, while the interior walls are lined with moabi panels.

The main task for the architect in this rehabilitation —apart from the technical problems —consisted in designing and organising the different spaces of the apartment, and resolving the problems of execution and assembly of the different materials. The absence of exposed fittings on the wall panels of the interior helps to enlarge and unify the volume of the main room, which opens on both sides onto a terrace of 50 square meters covered with a jatoba wood deck and offering spectacular views of the urban landscape.

The interior of this unusual dwelling is composed only of a living room with an open integrated kitchen, in which a chimney is framed between two shelves, and a small bedroom with its bathroom. This room enjoys the benefit of two sources of natural light that illuminate this more private area: a small window in the back wall and a skylight located over the bed. The floor of the interior is made of chestnut parquet covered with white polyurethane paint that reduces the colour saturation and brings freshness to the dwelling.

The wood, chosen for its plastic and structural qualities, is used as a double skin: soft and beautiful in the interior and rough and sturdy on the exterior. Thus, although this organic material is set against the urban nature of an environment in which steel is the main component, its form fits well into the geometric pattern of the building.

Photographs: Joel Cariou

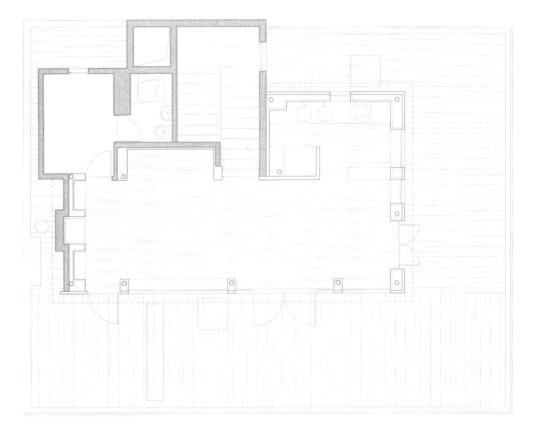

Claesson, Koivisto, Rune
Private apartment / Town house

Stockholm. Sweden

The team of architects Marten Claesson, Eero Koivisto and Ola Rune were reponsible for the work done in two apartments in the centre of Stockholm.

In the first one, for a young manager with little free time, they attempted to organize a small home to convert it into a peaceful space for "charging the batteries" after long working days and trips. It was decided to maintain half of the original —the living room— and to make all the other rooms —the bedroom, kitchen and bathroom— totally modern. The floor plan was devised in order to create visual fluidity between the rooms. To communicate the spaces in a simple and functional way, two new structures were designed. A curved corner leads from the entrance into the first axis along bathroom, kitchen and bedroom. The second axis of intersection runs from the kitchen to the dining room, where a wall with a hatch was built.

The final result was a spacious and comfortable apartment, full of light. The second scheme was set in a Neo-Classical building of the early 20th century. The client acquired the whole property and decided to remodel two of the flats to create his private dwelling; a bright apartment giving onto the garden.

The space had previously been occupied by a number of small dwellings and had undergone many changes over the years. To create a feeling of space, most of the walls were demolished, while the floors, the windows and the original radiators were conserved. One of the main interventions was the creation of a complex stairwell between the two floors, with glazed openings like those of churches. On the upper floor a major feature is the modern design of the bathroom, with a high bathtub designed by the architects and placed strategically to offer panoramic views of the port of Stockholm.

Town house

Private apartment

To make good use of the spaces the dishwasher, refrigerator and freezer are totally integrated behind the doors of the kitchen cupboards.

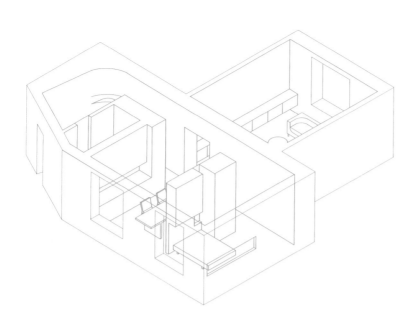

Town house

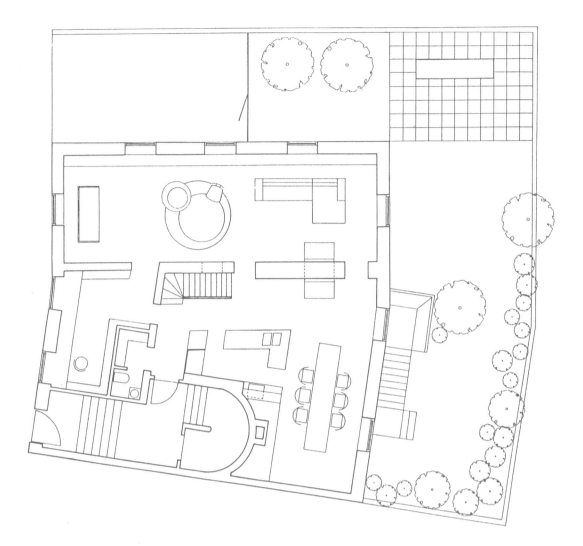

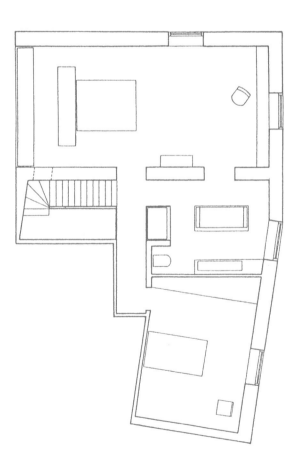

The geometry of this project is distinguished by simplicity and functionalism. The straight lines and the contrast between the different materials highlight the new volumes, giving the whole a modern appearance.

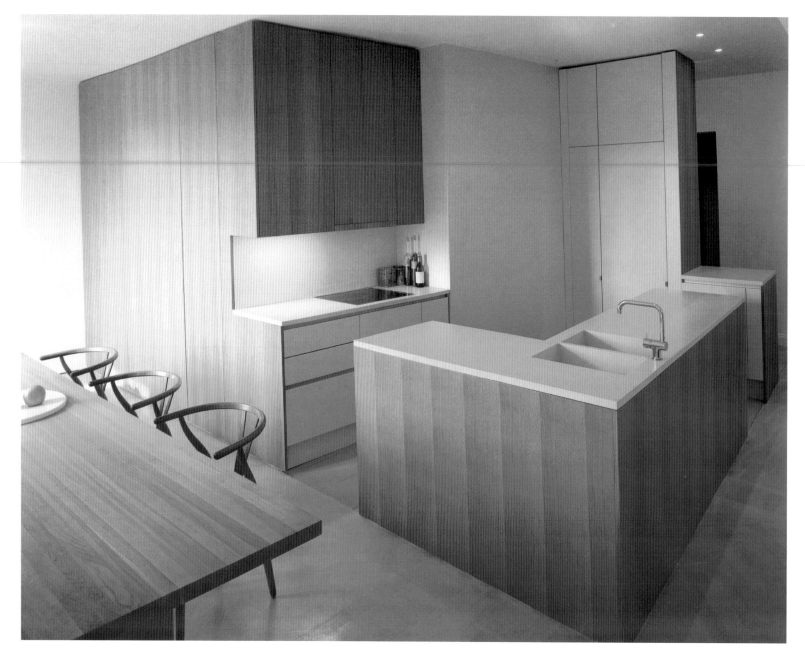

Mauro Galantino & Federico Poli (Studio3)
Casa sul lago d'Orta

Orta S. Giulio. Italy

This unusual building is located in the Gothic district of an Italian town not far from Milan. The vertical nature of the house is conserved almost intact thanks to the two medieval walls that define the boundaries and the jetty.

Before the restoration, the building was in ruins, the ceilings were deteriorated and a large part of the foundations rested on the sandy bed of the lake. According to studies that have been made, this building was partly rebuilt in the 14th century, though the jetty was built in the 19th century. At first sight, it seems to be a simple rehabilitation: a productive residential microcosm. The domestic areas, such as the bedrooms and the living room, are organised vertically in the north "tower", while below the former cowshed, the henhouse, the garden and the jetty are organised with reference to the lake. The restoration of this house —used as a second residence— respected the stipulations for the conservation of the cultural heritage with regard to volumes, walls and materials. The work was based on two objectives: to adapt the residential structure to new functions, and to obey the building regulations on the use of materials without sacrificing the possibility of a creating a new perception of the rehabilitated parts.

The result was a residential space composed of a living room of double height forming a horizontal, parallelepiped space with a covered jetty at the south end and a "tower" containing the living areas at the other end.

The staircase communicates the floors of the "tower" located at the north end of the residence which houses the bedroom. At the south end is the jetty giving onto Lake Orta.

Nick McMahon
66 St. John Street

London. UK

St. John Street is situated in one of the few areas of remaining historic fabric within London. It is fast becoming an area for high quality city dwelling, as the area acquires new restaurants, bars and shops. These new amenities in conjunction with its geographical location, only minutes away from the city, make this a totally appropriate living environment. The other important characteristic of this area is that during the day it is busy and industrious, but in the evenings and weekends the area is remarkably free of traffic and noise, as it is not a route between any significant vehicular destinations. This means that the area affords peace and quite, when the apartments are most heavily used. The principle objective of the scheme is to provide comfortable, unique city apartments which optimise the amenities of the building and the city, large areas of terracing and a flexible structure in terms of loads and cutting of holes.

Given a clearly ordered three dimensional structure, the objec-tive was to establish a system for using the existing and extending its potential by layering and cutting. The ambition was to create a collection of unique apartments that at the same time inextricably belong to each other as the collection that defines the whole.

The resulting scheme consists of self-contained dwelling units generated by applying a process of walls on diagonal and orthogonal girds to the existing envelope, thereby breaking down the strong existing order and allowing space to crystallise within the given three dimensional restraints. This solution produced a reduction of common parts and a series of 14 different units defining a three dimensional puzzle that can be assembled in only one way to fit within the existing external envelope and structural grid. The units are one and two storey and where these volumes meet the facade they are expressed in the fenestration, enabling the internal complexity to read through the ordered facade.

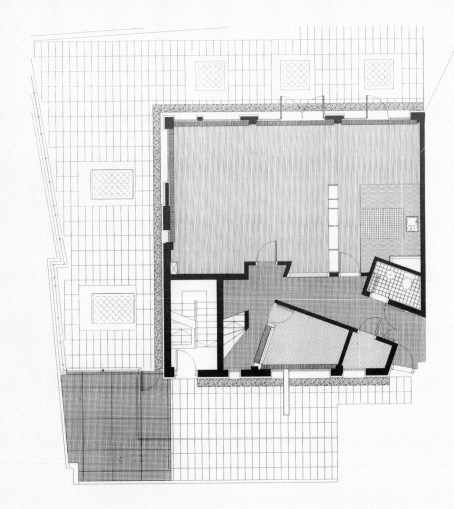

The resulting scheme consists of large unique dwelling units generated by applying a process of walls on diagonal and orthogonal girds to the existing orthogonal envelope, thereby breaking down the strong existing order and allowing space to crystallise within the given three dimensional restraints.

eok: eichinger oder knechtl
Monocoque, Wohnung Schretter

Vienna. Austria

This former laundry attic room has been converted into a 35 m², fully equiped loft. Apart from the separate 15 m² bedroom, all basic functions are housed in a "multidirectional unit". One wall has been removed and the roof structure has been covered with meral and plasterboard. Additionally, part of the exterior garret wall has been replaced with a large, two-part, movable glass construction.

Inside the heavy metal, front security door is a large cupboard which acts as a translucent room-divider and houses the washing machine and control unit for all functions within the loft, operable by remote control. In the evening it transforms into a huge lamp. The lavatory is located at one end of the cupboard, separated by stainless-steel doors that allow access from both sides. These can be closed in front of the lavatory pan so that it disappears into its own storage unit, hidden in a tiny space and leaving a path through the cupboard.

Alternatively, a larger, luxurious space can be created. The path through the cupboard allows access to the kitchen, which is lined by a net wall on one side and the cupboard on the other. Behind the net is the sink, enclosed in a glass cube. The net wall can be folded to create a shower cubicle, its fittings concealed and integrated into a metal column. In the shower area, the black "sickaflex" gaps in the American oak yatch floor have been routed to form a water drain.

Once the net wall is folded the other way, the shower and sink are concealed, leaving no clue that they exist. It is therefore possible to allow snow to enter the room, creating a particular ambient in certain occasions.

The large, two-part window is electrically operated. Part one tilts upwards until it reaches a height of 2.10 metres. Part 2 is operated separately and slides outside along the concrete unit, creating a balcony surface that extends the size of the room.

Photographs: Margherita Spiluttini; eok

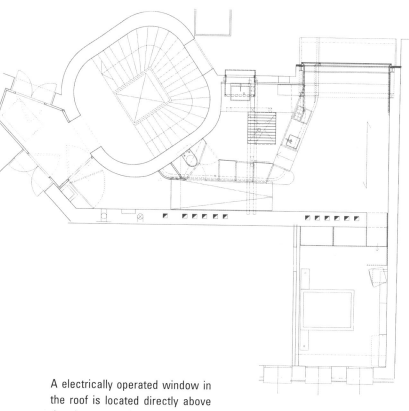

A electrically operated window in the roof is located directly above the shower, so that the occupant can also wash directly in the snow or rain.

Andrea Modica
Duplex in Milano

Milano. Italy

The space occupied by this dwelling was formerly a palace used as a congress hall, which explains the large windows in the walls.

The building was divided into small and austere apartments, but has maintained its distinctive appearance within a very bright environment.

The daring orange colour of the long walls stands out against the dull, neutral colours that predominate in the rest of the dwelling. So as not to interrupt the large windows in the single space of only 32 sqm, a mezzanine was created for the bedroom and the dressing room, providing almost 21 sqm more for the night area. This space is accessed by a spiral metal staircase located against the coloured wall that avoids the excessive presence of strong colours.

The brightness of this apartment corresponds to the Nordic taste of its owners, so there are no curtains or blinds on the windows. Thus, the horizon is free and the house is always flooded with natural light.

The floors of the whole dwelling, including the bathroom, were designed with bleached fir floorboards measuring 20 cm wide and up to 4 m long.

The kitchen is delimited by the space of made-to-measure cabinets by the interior designer in MDF, a material composed of panels of wood fibre and resin that is very strong and knock-proof.

The dressing room is just behind the bedroom and is accessed through two small openings located symmetrically on both sides of the bed, protected only by fine translucent drapes.

Fotografías: Giulio Oriani. Vega MG

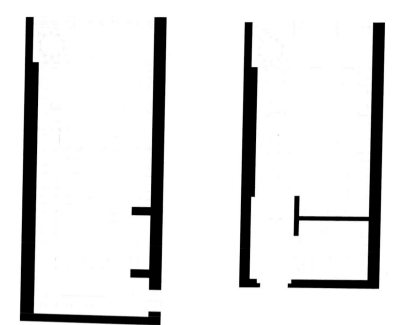

Ove Rix
House in Arhus

Arhus. Denmarck

Beautifully situated on a slightly canting landscape with small islands, which ends out in the open sea, this is a 1904 holiday home bought and renovated by the architect for his own use. The building is situade on a small hill, with a splendid view over Arhus bay, looking towards Helgenaes. From almost all arond the house, there is air and water.

The renovated exterior has the features and materials of a typcal Danish house, but this traditional appearance contrasts sharply with the atmosphere of te completely transformed interior whose rooms, once relatively closed and introspective, are now more open to the sea and the unspoilt natural surroundings.

The new layout has created communicating spaces around the new stairwell. Simple custom-built furniture combines with bright gloss colours -inspired in the nature- which artist emil Gregesen has skilfully made into a graphic feature of the interior design.

"The first owners' demands were different. They wanted a closed house, but we have, with great respect for the original house, "dared to open it more towards nature" says Ove Rix, "now when you sit inside the house, you really feel like you are in nature".

As seen on this page, generous glazed openings expose the dwelling to the sea and surrounding nature. The fireplace separates the kitchen from the living room.

Fabienne Couvert & Guillaume Terver
Villa les Roses

Aix-en-Provence. France

This dwelling, built in the fifties, is an inhabitable pavilion of 60 square meters located at the entrance to a forest in the north-west of Aix-en-Provence that has been declared a protected area. As the regulations of the area only permitted the construction of 30% of the plot, the old garage had to be rehabilitated and enlarged to respond to the new needs of the clients, a couple with two children.

The dwelling has a living room, kitchen, bathroom, scullery, office and two bedrooms. This scheme thus responds to two seemingly contradictory requirements: to allow each room to

work independently without this being a nuisance, and to maintain a large fluidity between the spaces.

The distribution of the functional programme is governed by two perpendicular elements that allow the space to be occupied. The first element consists of a technical block housing the kitchen, the scullery, a toilet and a bathroom. The second element is formed by a functional block housing the cupboards, a mobile partition and an office. The doors and woodwork were made in okume plywood.

The use of mobile elements such as the wooden panels that connect or isolate the kitchen from the dining/living room provides total flexibility and versatility in the use of the space, creating atmospheres that adapt easily to the most immediate necessities of the occupants.

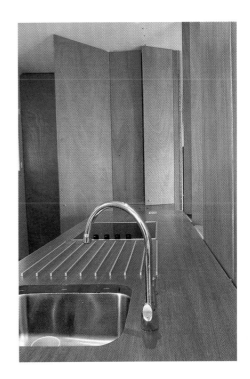

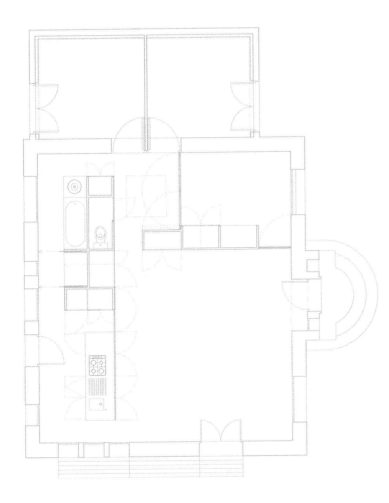

José Gigante
Wind Mill Reconverting

Vilar de Mouros/Caminha. Portugal

In the grounds of a recovered house in northern Portugal, an old abandoned windmill waited its turn to be useful again. In the course of time the idea finally arose of transforming this peculiar building into a small auxiliary dwelling belonging to the main house, giving it its own life and thus creating a completely inhabitable and independent space that could be used as a place of rest. For José Gigante, the architect in charge of the conversion, the presence of the mill was so strong that any major intervention would have minimised its charm. Therefore, without touching any of the thick granite walls, an unusual cooper roof with a very gentle slope was added. The intention was to respect the memory of the place as far as possible, so the inspiration for the transformation began naturally from the inside towards the outside. The layout and organisation of the small space, with only eight square metres per floor, was not easy. Thanks to the choice of wood as the main building material, a welcoming atmosphere enhanced by the curved walls and the few openings was achieved. On the lower floor, an impressive rock acts as an entrance step. On this level it was attempted to achieve a minimum space in which it was possible to carry out different activities. It houses a bathroom and a living room, with the possibility of transforming a small sofa into a curious bed: it is conceived as a case that contains all the necessary pieces for assembling the bed. On the upper floor, the furnishings are limited to a cupboard and a table/bed that is extended to the window.

The only openings are those that already existed in the mill and they have been left as they were conceived, with their natural capacity to reveal the exterior and to illuminate a space in which the contrasts between the materials cannot be ignored. The typology of this building was crucial to the restorations to which it has been subjected, and shows why the interior space is so important in this scheme. The thick circular walls occupy more space than the interior of the mill, but they hug the whole room and provide a welcoming and unconventional sensation that give this building a new and innovative perspective.

Photographs: Luis Ferreira Alves

To solve the problem of the lack of space, a system was devised in which a bed is hidden at the foot of the staircase.

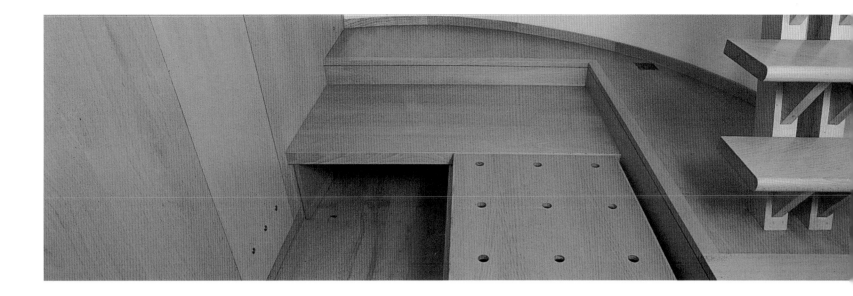

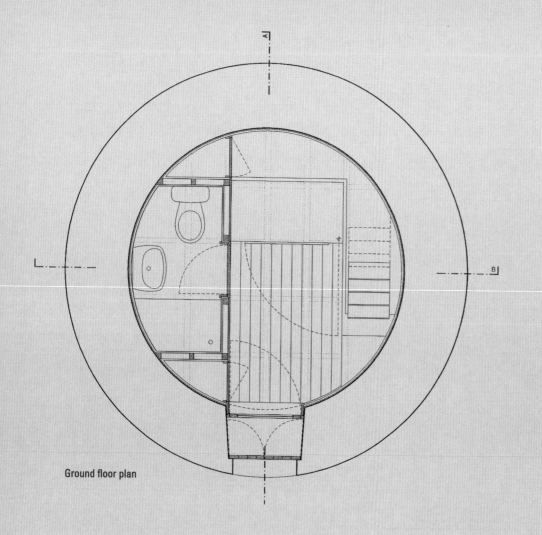

Ground floor plan

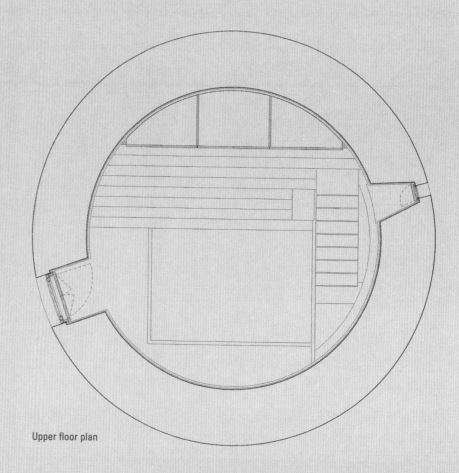

Upper floor plan

Brookes Stacey Randall
Lowe apartment

London. UK

Brookes Stacey Randall were commisioned to provide a "calm light interior space" within the top small floor of a converted warehouse.

The form of the existing shell was a very particular half arch with a small side space. A potential roof terrace was separated from the main volume and accessed via a lower terrace and a spiral staircase.

The main volume was treated as a room whose function can change depeding on the particular facilities brought into use.in order to achieve this, the small side space was split into storage and bathroom areas. The storage area was equipped with three large pull-out "pods", each providing a different faclity for the main space.

Each pod was designed to cantilever out on a triple extending mechanism, similar to that of filing cabinet drawer.

Directly above the centre of the space, a curved double glazed rrflight opens on hidraulic rams.

The circulation within the flat has been designed to maximise a sense of scale, concealing views and revealing them as the user moves through the space. The convergent curved wall lead the user from thc dim entrance toward the light of the main space whilst the route broadens and the height increases towards the the curved ceiling rising above.

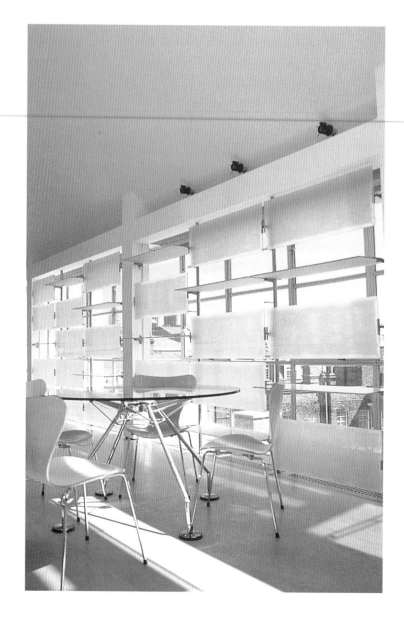

Photographs: Katsuhisha Kida

The staircase built totally in structurally resistant glass is designed to be as light and transparent as possible to avoid interrupting the visual continuity of the space.

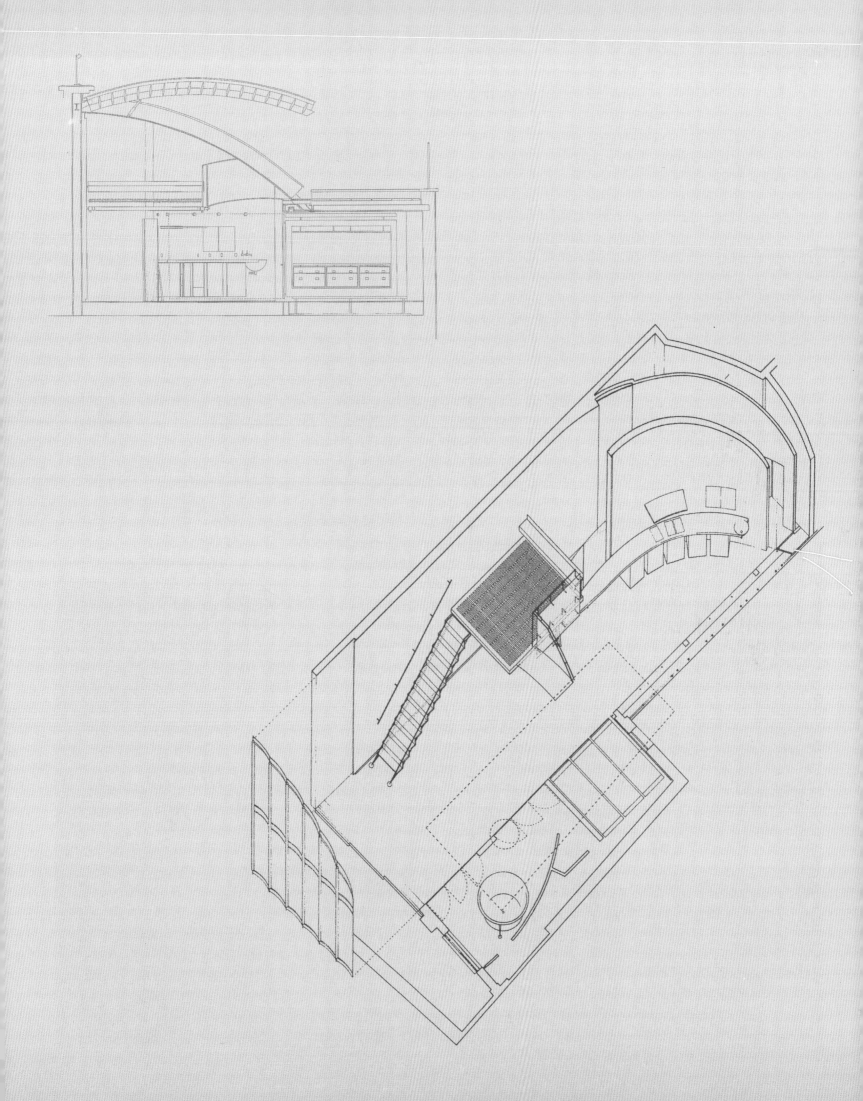

Philip Gumuchdjian
D.P. Think Tank / Boathouse

Skibbereen, Country Cork. Ireland

Set into the River Ilen in west Ireland, the building was conceived as a retreat for a famous film producer.

The architecture reflect a wide range of references: boathouse structures, barns, cow sheds, chlets, and a European perspective on Japanese pavilions. The building resolves these references into a simple expression of frame, rof and screens.

The dominant element of the design is the overhanging roof structure wich provides physical and psychological protection from the considerable annual rainfall.

A clear hierarchy of architectral elements (roof, structure, screens and glazing) was crucial to creating its legibility as an apparently enclosed "found" structure —a simple and timeless object. Transparency and perforated screens were deployed to keep the building open to the elements but also frame views and suggest enclosure and protection.

The materials of the structure are selected to juxtapose "stable" elements such as glass and stainless steel against the highly "changeable" and weathering materials of the cedar roof planks, slats and decks and the iroko frame. Set against the vivid colours and reflections of the site —green fields, blue/silver river, dramatic blues and greys of the sky— the silver of the building permanently changes colour as roof and structural frame become wet during showers and bleached under the sunshine.

174

A long pier extends the house onto the river, creating a space for escape and a perspective from which the interior of this small dwelling can be appreciated.

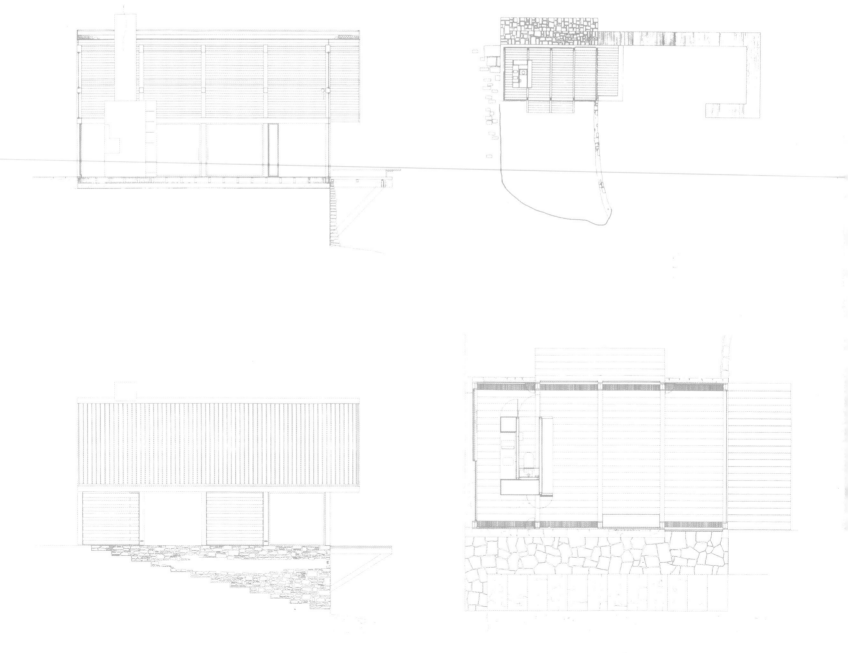